dust or fire

ALYDA FABER

dust or fire

icehouse poetry
an imprint of Goose Lane Editions

Edited by Ross Leckie.
Cover and page design by Julie Scriver.
Cover illustration adapted from *Dybbølsbro Station* by SirPecanGum, flickr.com (CC BY-SA 2.0).

Printed in Canada.
10 9 8 7 6 5 4 3 2 1

Library and Archives Canada Cataloguing in Publication

Faber, Alyda, 1963-, author
   Dust or fire / Alyda Faber.

Poems.
Issued in print and electronic formats.
ISBN 978-0-86492-922-8 (paperback).--ISBN 978-0-86492-942-6 (epub).--
ISBN 978-0-86492-943-3 (mobi)

   I. Title.

PS8611.A23D87 2016   C811'.6   C2016-902438-5
                                          C2016-902439-3

We acknowledge the generous support of the Government of Canada, the Canada Council for the Arts, and the Government of New Brunswick.

Goose Lane Editions
500 Beaverbrook Court, Suite 330
Fredericton, New Brunswick
CANADA E3B 5X4
www.gooselane.com

In memory of my mother and father,
Jacoba Faber Houtsma and Pieter Faber.

That flesh is but the glass, which holds the dust
That measures all our time

— George Herbert, "Church Monuments"

Contents

Unsaying Poems

Jealousy

Hy mei it net lije dat de sinne yn it wetter skynt.

I had the misfortune
to be raised in a snake family
the father all jaws and stomach
long-nosed for frog hunting.

Like the despot
of a small country
his name is whispered,
his teeth grind every tongue.

Try to own a small corner
the nose finds its way in.
And the father-enigma drops
la jalousie down on my soul again —

he doesn't want the sun
to shine on the water.

Cactus Essay

Byn it dy om de knibbel, dan slacht it dy net om it hert.

i.

On bright grass, the dead squirrel like a fur-cup,
its rib unfurls out of a minute red sea.

My mother lies in the hills, box-sealed from pain.
Out of my vision, now she lingers in my throat.

In an Ontario gothic farmhouse, my mother remade
Dutch windows she left behind. Succulents tangled
in dusty friendliness. One winter she grew cacti from seed,
wood heat and morning sun warming cloudy tents.

If she'd met my father's family before the wedding
she wouldn't have married him, my mother often said,
but never told us of the conference of three,
her parents' doubts pared down by her keen love.

Then a late summer ocean voyage to in-laws,
food put to combative uses, basket greens
of madness, wallpaper bullet wound,
no-turning-back pregnancy.

Remembering this is like opening the cellar door in spring,
beneath the kitchen tiles dark water rises to the third step.

Bind your grief under your knee

ii.

A nurse says my mother is dehydrating naturally. A week to dry out
and then she begins to bleed. Waters of veins and arteries leak
from the intestinal tract. Red weeping
cannot be stopped on that last night of clicking breath.

After fights, my mother would sit at the kitchen table long
into the night, turned into that secret place
she said a married woman
must reserve for herself.

Years later, she told me about chest pain and arm pain,
and conflict. *If I die, I could get out of here.*
She left one summer to live with her sisters in Holland
and, returning, said, *marriage is for life.*

A March visit to the doctor, her usual preparations neglected,
wearing a crumpled print dress, smelling like overripe cheese.
In the hospital lounge she touched my amber earrings
and said, *I am almost down the drain.*

Bind your grief under your knee and it won't rise

iii.

Trees tell light.
If only we could marry trees.

My father found my mother lying in the yard
under the maple tree, wearing a T-shirt and underwear.
The feed man arrived.
They carried her into the house.

Three days later her eyes drift over me
as if watching from the bed of a fast-moving stream.
Her words roll out over stones.
Under water, maybe I could understand.

Cacti still occupy the north and west windowsills.
On the floor, a cactus my mother grew from seed.
Its fleshy stem strains against ceiling tile and plaster,
reaching as if believing in a desert.

Bind your grief under your knee and it won't rise to your heart

In my mother's last days her flesh recedes —
tree sculpted bone.

Topsy-Turvy

It is der alhiel holderdebolder.
Always topsy-turvy here.

She called it the household of Jan Steen
and there on the Rijksmuseum wall
dogs and people in a tangled
mess and pots boiling over
and somewhere in a corner someone
has a psyche with no gates —
a person bent over with
socks half off and eyes sunk
down to his kidneys.
The entry gapes. No resistance —
it's already patterned
and you're there without
knowing there or here
or me or you in that
interior household
without
advantage
of standing back,
looking,
without chiaroscuro.

Inner Tube Run

Sy kin net fan it aai ôfkomme.

A child watches other children sliding away
from her over the edge
of the round hill.
Their faces reappear
and disappear again.
She's held back
from plunging into a deep
white sea with them
on rudderless inner tubes,
weightless speed.

The sinking children throw
laughter back up the hill
but she hears a dirge
and waits
until the sun tilts
and tree shadows stretch
out long in the fields.

She can't get off the egg
until another child lures her
into a squeaking black boat
over the edge
and down.
Icy whirling wind
and gentle spin.

Grace Unwitting

Dêr't de hûn syn sturt leit, is it skjinfage.

If God writes
with a child-thick marker. . .

> Note this — bones
> in sockets rotating, inner folds
>   digesting, electrical
>   fields balancing, vast interior
>   surfaces thrumming on —

but on *our* surface
so much debit accounting —
ink gauged,
lines measured
exact, one thin-skinned tit
scratched on another's tat —

> But note this
> *where the dog's tail lies*
> *the floor is swept clean.*

Treading Ox

De swarte okse hat dy noch net op de foet west.

i.

At nine years this is her experiment.

Earth's hardback trod by cows, cars, tractors, milk trucks,
open sun outside the tree-surrounded house yard
beyond the barn yard's fenced peak of manure.

Her uniform the required dress — girls wear dresses.

The driveway's hard surface cants
as she tests the learned familiars —
this is my body   these my hands   this my face.

Who *am* i?   *Who* am i?   Who am *i*?
One question asked and asked and asked
rips down shelves holding things
used to saying i am:

falling clay pots, boxes with last year's seed packets,
torn tops folded down, dirt-caked gloves' crooked fingers.

Sun lances the sky, wrongness feels right.

Why here looking out —
these feet, these arms?
Why this brain thinking behind these eye sockets?

Who thinks this body that others know
and call variations on a name?
Why do they think they know her when the familiar seal

holding the envelope this body this brain
can be slit open
exposing the private letter?

What do they know when they say
the black ox hasn't trampled on your foot yet?

ii.

   An unread letter opened other places too:
Sunday-after-church,
parents having coffee with parents,

children scattered in the house. She stops midway
in a room with oak mouldings, brick fireplace,
face pointed to the dining room table, some chairs askew,

legs inches from the deep sofa where her mother's nyloned ankles
and Sunday-shoed feet are entwined.
Not knowing how to act in company

stops her — her lack of polite questions — stops her.

She doesn't know how long she stands there.
Wills herself into motion, enduring
another twist of the hidden corkscrew.

Chaste

In soad wurden folje gjin sek.

A man, let's call him Door.
That quaint impossibility
a look sealed.

More looks, trembling hand on coffee cup,
more impossibility.
All on my side.

Those sensual autumns
unwanted chasteness.

Interior so lit up, the running
landscape dark and unreadable.
Words won't fill a sack.
Bushels of words even.

Door wouldn't come closer
when my conflicted limbs and bones and kidneys
said   dont touch dont touch dont touch
even as their needle-thin mewling says   touch.

War Questions

Hy sjocht as in kat yn de foarke.

Questions slide fingers
under an arm's pale
frog thigh   Clenched
tobacco lid pulled
open   roll out stock pieces

He's in the passenger seat
I'm driving   each query
drawing out a bare answer
from the interrogation chair
Splintery obedience

*He looks like a cat caught
in pitchfork tines*
Cannot tell his distress
Sits unmoving, his hand
cutting an angle across

his chest   and a sound
like low tired exhalation
Fear of being shot
he doesn't say
Guilt leaving his father

he doesn't say
Returning home without
his father   he doesn't say
Lost respect   he says
Lost respect how   I want
to know what that means
I don't ask

Escape from Germans
in his socks   klompen kicked off
Running across a beet field
Escape socks Germans beet field
Socks beet field escape Germans

All these years alone in the story
This telling he and his father
captured by Germans rounding
a corner in the village one year
before war's end   Beginning

of his father's bitter cinders
Marched in file with neighbours
and a neighbour's hired
hand to a hotel
in the next village

His only chance for escape
outside the village
Kicking off his klompen
and his father he ran
into the beet field

In a camp near
the German border
prisoners dug tank traps
to keep the Allies out of Holland
His father never the same
The neighbour's hired hand
dead soon after war's end

Paperpants

As myn broek in pipersek is.

When my pants are a paper bag I'll use them to make lists — elegant things, distressing things, and best of all, things that "quicken the heart." A famous list-maker, Shonagon, lady-in-waiting to Sadako, recommends this. Elegance: grass bending in the wind, sunlight paddling through windy leaves, unarmoured reply to a guns-out blazing meanness, kindness moored on the ancient saying, *be kind — everyone you see is fighting a great battle.*
Distress: the long aftermath
of a death, wishing
dead the undead parent,
wishing alive the dead
parent, the rages of an
infernal father hiding
love under piles of bones
for a bitter game of
hide-and-go-seek-and-
never-find until the
corners of the room
begin to whiten out
in the psychiatrist's
three-chaired bare
office, breathing
two arm-lengths
from clasping eyes.

A quickstep heart:
love like those feet
that stop and wait
and look at a starling
tacked to a sidewalk
by blood leaking
from the beak, its free
wing making a flap
flap flap, that staring
admission to her usually
well-hidden interior — *het
ontroerde mij* — "it stirred me
when you...." Velázquez's
Lady with a Fan — her eyes
backlight the sternum,
set the torso humming,
a twin-engine ready
to take off — *where?*

Mole-Sick

Sjen foar eagen is gjin gûchelspul.

in our family's underground world
the tunnelling began early
detecting by feel not ask

vestigial eyes   tentacle-like nose
forage under grassy skin

an "eye doctor" treats
our uncle's surfeit
visions and voices

we assail each other
home   the anxious nest
summer and winter
treading soil   treading sediment bottoms
of ponds and streams hidden
in cedar swamplands
sharp quick nerve for our prey

elusive grey pelt
rudimentary eye

seeing is no conjurer's game

our father's months of paranoia
a "sunstroke"

death fingering him daily
full chorus singing non-stop insults in all keys
heart doing double time
hands idle

burrowing
into borrowed
sensation
we tunnel around each other

Three Old Frisian Sisters

In healjier is net oan de stôk bûn.

i. Siem

Wheeled into the garden, her dementia cuts corners.
"I am that ruined house."

Roll up the table carpet.
Dense pile swallows dishes, ornaments.

Viscous red on brown, liquid column of white —
we're stranded here — wedged into a mutely staring supper.

Coffee grinders hole-punch a patina sky.
Just try tying a year to a stake.

Llamas and goats graze a circumference.
Strolling shrubs, roosters and hens.

Hedges list toward sea-battened windows.
Turn down turn down the volume on the ocean floor.

ii. Tjits

Time, you old shuffler, where's the ambler gone?
The body's casualties pile up.

TV anchors converse in the living room.
Evening strollers wander through the hall.

Tick-burr heart and sugar-steeped blood
too much psychic traffic on twisted feet.

Children, come to her lonely supper.
Red plastic chairs, beaming metal legs await.

Her muffin orphaned between ordering and arrival.
A year cannot be bound to a stake.

Feet distress the stairs.
These young strangers — why are they here?

iii. Jacoba

Rain slicks the hair when she lives in a downpour.
War in the windows again.

Torso juts out of the wood fire.
A tarp once covered legs imperfectly, nothing to hide.

Day leapfrogs night, gnaws on sleepfolds.
Orange ghosts rib the cactus plant.

Knots will slip from a year tied to a stake.

An anxious button nictitates.
Orotund voices scatter words off a shelf.

Memory pills ransack flesh —
nausea, crimping muscle, fatigue, oh anorexia.

Wind carts her hydrangea hair into strangers' gardens.
What is the sky thinking?

The snapper swan commingles with Leda again.
What are we humans doing below?

The Ones You Believe

Alle geasten moat men net leauwe.

don't believe all spirits
just the ones

whose white hot teeth
afflict your spine

so you cannot
sit   stand   run

you burn cold

trying to find
love's temperature

The Visit

Kom ik by dy, ús Heare God sil net by dy komme.

The crow flies
at the passenger side
of the car, braking
tail and accelerating wings.

Other crows carve rough
openings in a sky turned
on the horizon
like a screw-top lid.

My *bestemming*, my father.
Bestemmen, to intend.
My will says no my flesh says yes.

*

Family voices begin to ride
my roller-coaster spine
through one- and two-stoplight towns.

      Internally exposed to the elements —
his house —
my liver revolts.

I may visit you, but I'm not God.

*

We drive further north
to the Mennonite for eggs, and after
visit my old catechism teacher. Chess pieces
at the table, we hear his story
of depression and its shame dogs.

My father shrunk
in a chair looks at fly specks
on the window.

Almost inaudible —
the soul's creaking.

*

The prophet tells King David,
lately returned from Bathsheba mourning
her husband just killed on front lines:

A rich man, his backyard filled with sheep,
takes a poor man's only lamb.
Like a daughter, it used to lie in his bosom,
drink from his cup. Faced with David's rage,
the prophet says,
                        You are the man.

*

What insular theft
turned my father thief?
Who taught him to see life
as a God-slot where sin
must be paid and paid?

*

Bending
to my side of the car, one last lesson —
you've got to forgive — did my catechism
teacher say this?

*

The beeping fire alarm doesn't need batteries.
Light a match under —

it shrieks.

Looks

Sy sjocht as in brette ûle yn de tange.

Those looks that can't be classified.

No typology, no phases of the moon
can explain them.

    A look that travels through the circus rings
of scalp and shoulders and triangle
of trapezius, that crinks the bowel,
that has the rider adrenal
gland kicking the kidney.
      The look of an owl
      roasting in the tongs.

A look Rembrandt in the Frick flings you,
self-portraiture a criss-cross of straining lines
in beefeater and fur and red sash and ochre,
face framing the livid cave of his eyes.

On Not Dying

In minske kin de waarme siel net behâlde.

There is no such thing as dying
Augustine says in *City of God*
puzzling where living becomes dying.
When you are still living you are not
dying but living until the moment
you are dead
and then you are not dying either
but dead.

He wondered too about the sundering
of body and soul formed in such intimacy
that the two are pulled apart
anguish grating
violin strings of the flesh
every bit of light and slices of dark.
The impossibility
of holding onto the warm soul.

Eulogy

Lit de dief eat oer, de brân lit neat oer.

I often felt
turpentine hatred
cut with liquid horror.
A hidden love distilled.

I often wished
he lay dead before me
and now
antiseptically he does.

I rehearse a eulogy
for a theft and a fire.
The thief leaves something
but the fire leaves nothing.

Leeuwarden Train Station

Leeuwarden Train Station

Six years after my mother's death, I ask my father about their first meeting.

Treeless gaunt, pleated into dirt-filled crevices, in one part of the story his eyes and voice sent a flare across the table: she caught me, she grabbed hold of me — words the word "hug" cannot translate.

She answered his ad in the newspaper: correspondent wanted by soldier, homesick, military service in Indonesia.

They met at the train station because she couldn't bring anyone to the house. Her twenty-three-year-old sister had just died.

How her parents trusted him to take her to Canada.

She grabbed hold of him, and he would never let her go.

When we were very small, he would carry us under his arms like canvas rolls to the front stoop, along planks lined up over a muddy yard. For many more years, he would grab hold of us when the devil had a pitchfork up his ass.

When I visit him, his greetings are concise: oh, it's you.

In more expansive moods, his greetings touch upon clothes: he recalled that his mother always referred to people wearing shorts as white sticks; he asked, *do you know what a man said to a soldier? You can fill your boots with poop.*

His hammer, his children the nails.

My father walks with two canes, head down, grimy yellow cap a hungry beak pecking at the sidewalk. I open the car door, will close it when he is inside, will drive him anywhere he wants to go, will sit for hours in his kitchen until the light falls gray, but I do not touch him.

His helplessness attracted your mother. She was a martyr, my aunt said.

In my mother's grief fog, was the stranger she held on a terminating or a through platform?

If I can believe a star chart made by a Vietnamese Buddhist I met at a gym (he was accurate on other points) then one of my parents was sex-obsessed.

If my brother remembers this accurately, he found a flat package under the mat in the car while waiting for our father in the laundromat. It was quickly snatched from his hand when he waved the shiny square in the sun falling on the churning machines.

Was it delectable, the child's bum he spanked red? A show, his gestures clown large, folderol laughter, I was the audience or in the ring, pants and underpants pulled down, teeter tottering across his lap. A circus for the very young.

How edible, children at any age. Still the child at any age.

The marriage pledge held my mother.

My father made solitary day trips to farmers' trade shows, returning late at night.

She grabbed hold of him, skirted by love she didn't feel for other suitors.

Only death did part them.

He bought three plots in the cemetery because he didn't want anyone near her.

When I was twenty-two, my uncle drove me to Amsterdam and said goodbye outside the train station. His hands cupped my face; he looked intently at me — the gesture seemed important so I remembered it, but I felt outside its meaning.

My uncle's only daughter, born three months and ten days after me, lived five years and 271 days.

My cousin sometimes fell down in the hall just after she got out of bed. And then the Hong Kong flu.

That same winter, a girl in my kindergarten class died. I saw the empty box where her things used to be stored. My mother saw me as the next fish to be caught on the fishing line, and ever after I ate with her sharpened knife and fork.

Living with those two ageless five-year-olds fills my tracks in snow.

For years, I feared that reaching look of my aunt and uncle.

In the hall of my apartment, my uncle reached out and kissed me on the lips, my body folding in awkward angles away from him. My aunt cut in sharply, *Zij kan daar niet tegen — you're upsetting her*.

Waiting on the station platform, the proximity of wheeling life and the still life.

Not the life my mother wanted, but she had days of the sun falling on her just so.

Not the father I wanted, but the one my mother greeted at the station and followed to Canada.

Just once I visited my cousin's grave, my uncle silent, walking ahead of us, my aunt talking — the many children who died that week, the doctor who said he would quit if one more child died — my uncle walking ahead in silence.

I could not venture any children into the world.

After a week away, in the hall with a suitcase, my cat greets me with a trill; I hold her close and kiss her. I do not do this instinctively with family.

My mother greeted him, and clasped him tight, the moment that decided him.

I find my father, in a red-checkered jacket and baseball cap, seated alone, in the back pew at the wedding. To my question, *do you want to move closer to the front?* he replies, *are you ashamed to sit with me?*

Is there any appetite so green as a child for a parent and so furious when the eyes of the room stare back empty?

There are so many moments before and after any photographic record when something in the flesh clicks open an aperture. My uncle and I sit on the black leather sofa looking at photos, a final act before the train station. When I close the small album, he turns to me and touches my face as if he could trace the ravenous child in the grown woman. As if the serviceable wings of a bee became a blur.

When my father thinks my visit is coming to an end, he turns to the pine trees bordering the lane and thanks me.

When my visit has really come to an end, he sits slumped in a chair by the wood stove. I walk across the gravelled vacant lot of my father. With store and gas pumps gone, no one plans to build.

My uncle cannot leave my aunt for very long — she may wander out into the street. From the train station, in too little time, the Atlantic between us again.

Only forest, fields, highways, lakes, towns and cities separate me and my father.

My father cannot let my mother go around the corner into her death.

About to drive into the glacial valley locals call the Hell Hills, my father asks — *did Mama and I take good care of all of you?* — a pause and then I say — *yes?*

Mid-afternoon traffic, sun glancing indifferently off metal and glass, my uncle tells me that they've had a Beetle and a Soviet car called the Ugly Duckling, small talk of departure right up to the automatic doors of the station.

As light fell in pearls, my mother held him, a stranger.

After my uncle's farewell, I watch from inside the station doors. I realize he's been sitting in his car a long time when he finally backs up and turns into the empty amphitheatre of the afternoon.

The train will leave on time.

I might walk through that meeting place, on my way to the train, where my mother held a stranger.

Still Life, Animal

Still Life: Reprise

Reclining on plush drapery

        the house a virgin, white trim

languorous green grapes

        on a blue habit. Rarely seen

blinking pomegranate winter seeds

        in public now, almost a visitation.

Lightly furred kiwi, arcing cherry stems.

        Down the dark hall of the window

dazzling on a royal apple, a fly,

        pleated light on a wall. Unseen

irreligious wings. A decanter,

        table holds a clear eddy,

eyeless eyes burst open manifold

        and, above, revolving red wheels

lintels in the splinter of the moment.

        Bloom.

Berlinale Erotik

Berlin Film Festival

i.

How did you find that film?

    My body liked it.

ii.

Day into night and night into day
revolutions repeated too quickly
for the eyes and the ankles,
theatre to theatre, film to film.
The dark outside
spinning spits of illumination,
a fast city on its way.
Airy golden mistletoe
orbiting street lights —
only the constellations along the aisles
not turning.

iii.

A Lego giraffe, two stories
of yellow and brown blocks
on the sidewalk near
curved walls of blue glass.
Its neck the length of an escalator.

iv.

Neon bracelets mark the Canadians
at the Canadian Embassy party.
We seem to be designated the ambassador's
friends — no one knows him in his own embassy
he says and tells us stories about George W. Bush.
In the small talk next to my friend's silvery brightness,
I emit a few sombre pulses. The ambassador
holds her hand a long while when saying goodbye.

v.

Meryl Streep receives an honorary Golden Bear,
thanking all the husbands and boyfriends
who accompanied their partners
to her films. She's not wearing stilettos;
her tall heels could walk across a lawn
without flinging her backwards.
She makes casual adjustments to her bust
as her Mrs. Thatcher does in *The Iron Lady*
and acknowledges that she gets all the glory
instead of directors and makeup artists.
The downside — in art galleries
people stare at her and ignore the paintings.

vi.

At the Gemäldegalerie I study Cranach's
Last Judgment triptych with another
anonymous patron. We find devils
horseshoeing people,
note the frequent body piercing
(a stake through the chest, a spear

through the back), a stove combusting
sinners, spiky creatures
in cartwheeling hells, green
the colour of monstrosity.
The scene that began it all, the left panel,
a high-altitude battle of insects,
black and white angels,
and down below, in a tree,
a mermaid serpent with breast implants
gives an apple to a feckless girl and boy.

vii.

Berlin's Erstes Erotik Labyrinth,
a darkened storefront
on Kurfürstenstrasse,
could have been a sign
on the cinema door.

viii.

The Tiergarten: rows of shirts with bold stripes
that yellow-cloaked birds dart between.
Grey column ribbed with gilded guns
raises a victory angel high above a traffic circle.
A philosopher seated on a colossal chair.
Pillar with busts of three composers,
topped with cupids dancing a laurel wreath,
and just below, swans with blackened wings
opened wide, their heads a lighter stone, cleft of war
damage visible on their outstretched necks.

ix.

Her face six stories high,
Queen L'Oréal looks down

x.

as her subjects leave and enter
the Potsdamer S-Bahn station,
a skitter of beetles.

xi.

Cranach's *Fountain of Youth*
an ex-carnival of old she-floppies
delivered in barrows and wagons
or on the arms of the young to a swimming pool,
where the gods Cupid and Venus stand on a pedestal.
Trained as we are to read left to right
and to wish away what can be read from the other direction —
the women are lowered gingerly into the waters
burdened with their slings of flesh, hesitant
and harried in their grey undress,
while on the other side, maidens
sport pink melamine mounds.
Young men appear in the scene
to catch the pond's young fish
once fully dressed for the table.

xii.

Such variable wants
as bodies jig puzzle sex
onscreen: post-hit-and-run,
initiation of a child soldier,
commercial trade, a nun's
and a priest's forgotten vows,
ripping-off-clothes-frenzy,
pulling-on-socks-sedate.
Try this piece, no that one,
a different angle,
no, yes, oh that's it
ease in and press down.

xiii.

An intimate dark with strangers.
All those exposed necks looking up.

xiv.

The actors set free from celluloid freeze
of storied movements:
calls from under a camera carapace
want to pin them again — a little to the right,
right — this way — left — middle — click, click,
clicking of jointed legs, wings scuffle.

xv.

The movies are mixed together
fast and freely like liquor
at a high-school party.
The new metal garbage can
takes vodka, rum, gin, wine into punch red
and trips the crowd from soft-petalled
romance to disaster
and back again.

xvi.

The sniffing nose of the kiss — for fun other body parts try.

xvii.

Lives onscreen larger than our kitchen sink,
human scrubbing
and no bits of soggy food.

xviii.

The films massage your waiting body,
take you into a stupor of rest
or press fingers so deep that nerves
diagram red hot.

Their mouths talk uneven tempos,
barnyard sparrows only louder,
browner, more teenager.

View of a Spring Evening between Porch Posts

Light moves each pleated leaf
as if parting the lips
before a word forms. Rustling

twilight. Early leaves trim
as bird claws, muted sharp
of children's voices at play.

She watches from the sofa.
His voice breaks in — *you get
such intensity because*

*primary colours of light
interact: red-orange sun,
the tone between blue-green and*

*yellow-green, a blue-violet
sky.* She looks into the room's
dimness where a shadow

lingers on the forgotten
rug. The wild rabbit in her,
tall in a cut hayfield,

towering ears, tremulous
tail, lowers its bone frame,
folds into a round of brown

fur. She's gone incognito,
all too readily her instinct.
What did you say? she asks.

Flesh-Ear

Listen to her

with your flushing blood
        pheromone rain bands
             vestigial tail
             solar plexus
      cruciferous bone
muscle fulcrum
face surface tension.

Hear what she's not-saying.
Hear what's in her, but not for telling.

Hear heat simmer over glitter-black shingles.
A scrim of mist on evening fields.

Goldfish

The shamelessness of goldfish
skimming the pond. Their fleshy Os

skirmish for flakes
dropped from a teaspoon;

among the reflected trees
flames flit in drowned wheels.

Was I once so round in expectation?
Mouth open for the nipple

breaking the surface of my own dark
without a glimmer of thinking.

Hoarfrost

i.

The hoarfrost shows
what you passed without seeing.

Here summer's webs hang,
random slings
under the tunnel's caged streetlights.

Trees clutch bone china
cups in the air
just for a morning.

Fog on the river;
God a guest
turning a doorknob.

ii.

The trees have fingers
and their touch
lays you
bare.

You a wick
to their flame.

You the vibrations
of their song.

ARoS Museum, Aarhus

Dante's rings of hell
form white stairwell rings
that leave you
at glass floor-to-ceiling doors.

Video of the cutting
up of a horse in an open field,
here in 112 jars
miniature landscapes inside glass,
archaeologies of red fur,
its windpipe, flesh, tubes, fat.

A crashed piano clings to tangled wires
dangling from cracked soundboard.
A man flees the apocalyptic music,
one leg frayed at the knee, an arm
in ribbons at the elbow,
capstans, whippens,
tuning pins
sunk in epoxy flesh.

Down into the innermost ring, a tall room;
if you step onto a grille, clasp the rails,
beside, over, under
are mirrored surfaces.

You free-fall into so many yous
and spin up into more.
Yes, I know this place.

Accept Loss

Greg Staats, triptych, black and white photographs (1995)

Excruciations

— twigs score
the heart, cut roots drip like taps.
Gone the plunder that built the sconce
yet a wedge of darkness lingers
in the people while ancestor
trees pinprick passing clouds, map
trails in dirt and lance festering
malignancies.

Muteness

Spirits straggle in compressed snow.
Domesticated mountain range
shifts under the fingered shadow
pouring over the horizon.
Above the reaching dark, silent threads
pray the sky empty, then scene change
for remote blankness over head
beyond ordering.

Mordant

A mouth that hides an inner roar —
Ontario gothic farmhouse.
Listen to windows and doors
for sleety keening without
beginnings and endings that bless.
Visible in unsettled foreground:
plowed field or grave, excavation mess
or memory mound?

Eucharist

After the snack-box children go inside,
    leaving mullion tracks in snow,
        see what ratcheters swooping from trees

uncover with their sooty beaks
    hidden in each wrapper,
        without giving thanks,

without kyrie eleison.

        What is left to the almost empty page?
            These discarded packets

that once held flakes of wafer.
    And what more can I want or know

        than this flying off after scavenging?

Saying Poems

On Looking Up into a Tree

Her leaves, upside-down
kitchen drawers.
Forks, knives, and spoons
hang bat-like,
all blue-tinged shine
and scant tinkle.

That's where
my love-hunger,
a ragged contagion
knotted into ropes,
coils among her root-hills
and looks up.

Her trunk's wary door
hides a stairwell
to a dizzy room.
When I'm there
walls sing me
happy absolution.

Death at Five Years

Nuzzling into her scant time on the ledger —
bright blocks, drawings large and bloomy,
page-cut and square bangs, eagerness

to grasp the tall broom and sweep. Pointed
and round red As, green Bs, yellow Cs
cross a corrugated blue wall

to a pair of pink Zs. Twelve train cars
rode five birthdays door to window —
for each, a different animal cake.

Stale cookies, apple-dented peanut
butter sandwiches, masking tape
names curled over coat hooks.

Carpet-level row of boxes
holds indoor shoes and treasures safe
for the 3:30 bell. Under a peeling

MARY ANN two rubber-soled navy
canvas shoes untouched from hand-me-down
snowsuits to spring squelchy boots.

Children wobble cups of red,
last-day-of-school treats, in a forest
of bare adult legs, skirts, flower-topped

sandals walking on nap-time rugs. Meshed
voices rise and fall, laughter darts between
gaps of talk. A woman in a green

shirtwaist dress clasps tight her buzzy
daughter's hand. Mary Ann's mother leans
toward them: "Can I look at your daughter?"

In the green mother's fluid fatalism,
a fear-pendulum starts up,
a bright echo at her side.

Trespassing

We went everywhere, easy
about crossing property lines
with our horses. We liked the look
of a neighbour's back field — asked permission
but he refused: *Haven't you got enough
land of your own to ride on?* We took down
part of the split-rail fence, rode Queenie
and Duchess over, circled the field,
closed the fence behind us, a door.
Periwinkle overgrown graves
near a Methodist Church, a rarely used
cottage now. Rooms like suitcases almost full
for tomorrow's travel. Or that house
being built near the lake. It was open
and we wandered through, imagined
furniture for the wide rooms, sat smoking
by the window cut-outs,
sun telegraphing water into flickering signals
in the tree leaves. We kept placing ourselves in larger
possibilities than we already knew.
An abandoned house, exposed
on a hill crest, alone on a stretch of road.
Above the doorknob, a padlock,
smashed with a rock until it released.
Inside our shoes made divots in the dust
in rooms left bare: a dead sparrow lay
on the floor in an upper room.
A girl's future could hold less
than the present moment:
windows open to sun and moon
would be boarded up, the interior dark
day and night. I couldn't see that then.

Redress

How natural an unhappiness

to be outfitted
    with mismatched parents.

How much
dressing and undressing
    in the brain drawers

before each parent
could appear
    unadorned human.

My Mother, Far and Near

i.

My mother's rage engine
walks out the door:

heat enough to take her
to the moon,
past the gateposts
where yesterday she held me
up to see a funnel spider.

Brothers rattle behind me.

Skin stings as the eldest grabs
my shoulders, pulls me
away from watching

her go.

ii.

Sun leans out of a waterless sky
as we pass the gateposts,
walk under the shushing pines.

Rivulets percolate under our feet
between bands of green.

Her anchoring arm guides my unsteady legs —
together we are joy —
riding winter's undoing.

iii.

Brought to her wordless deathbed,
staying in the night. Words that failed
us seventy times seven
have no betrayals left to renew —
old ones canker.

My cot, eye level
with her bed's machinery.

Spectral illumination from the hall —
elastic air
gathers us in.

This Love for Mother

Impossibly melted
twine in green glass,
a finger-ring suspends the toy's
clackers. Their tussive
coming together
fractures hunger.

Impossibly tangled
garter snakes in weave
of wintered grass and new spring.
One wraps a wrist, tongue
flashes a silent red, compressed
intestines unfed.

Impossibly late
snow falls in clumps, lighted ferries
foundering on dark pavement.
Breathed into strangers'
noses, riding on shoulders,
slow, damp, cold.

Impossibly thick
coffee, its bitter pleasure
now an emergency in
the churlish flesh engine.
A final swallow, grounds
between the teeth.

Suture

1. Surgery. joining the edges of a wound or incision by stitching; a seam or stitch made during this procedure; the material used to make surgical stitches

Those early morning calls, mother, you

ever sewn into my ligaments
insinuating as the living and more fleet.

Tease an oar through this lucid medium,
draw my sail, taut for absolution.

Throw out to sea all your flesh hooks,
ease the clamps on sinning selves.

Allow me to take a chance
with happiness, that depth charge.

2. the junction of two bones forming an immovable articulation,
especially each of the serrated borders between the bones of the skull

What the fields proffer
in their season
I still gather for you —

    this pleasure I permit myself.

On grass-bare earth a singsong of daisies.

Our long-gone house edged
by starred lilacs,
a green-wheeled spectre.

Hawthorn seedlings harbour
new forests under their spines.

    Silence hollowed us.
Without the cartilage of speech
we lived marrow and bone.
Could I have lured you
out from your hatched pencil lines

    and become unsheltered too?

3. Bot. & Zool. the junction, or line of junction, of contiguous parts, such as the line between adjacent whorls, chambers or valves of a shell, the seam where the carpels of a pericarp join

I regret
my unwillingness

for offspring.
Your bittersweet

motherhood
occluded

this desire. Certain
I could save you

from your life, I became
a maple ghosted

in your field,
roots exposed —

all those small
wind-trussed gestures
left undone.

4. Geol. the line of junction formed by the collision of two lithospheric plates

what drift is possible from you

so much adhesion under the skin

wanting your laughter to press my spinal ridges

a fiery igneous belt

kidney melding to spleen

our sometimes cloudless fusion

a bee forages a bristled globe thistle

your small frame lists to the left

*5. film. techniques used to obscure awareness that we are looking
with and through the camera at a story joined together from various
selected takes*

There is no release

           from everyday graceless cuts

yet love spools them along

           seamless across the lake.

Without upright features to offer resistance,

           a heavier wind and looser

scrolls white caps,

           spins near-shore rows of wind turbines.

Meditations on Desire

This desire glides
into winter harbour,
irreconcilable song
and lift of tropical
birds, all the heft
a container ship.
Words flit in colour
around the grey metal,
drop unheard, a
limp lustre of bodies.

A squirrel nearly hits you,
falling from a telephone wire
onto the sidewalk. Shakes
itself and scurries
up a nearby trunk. You're
unsure how much this desire
has left in it, after the ignition
of adrenalin. A full lifespan,
or a quick burn, hidden
up there in the leaves.

Light strands shuffle dune grass,
a kaleidoscope wobbles
between an illusion
of stable sand and ragged
drag and drift that goes on
as far as the eye can see.
This desire so large
a scope as a child running
the beach, into water,
all pink careening joy.

Birthday Call

I know the routine this call breaks into —
after dinner coffee on the black leather sofa.
My uncle's voice picks me up
and puts me down again,
he hands my voice to my aunt.
She's swimming in uncertain places,
a sieve my speaking pours through.
We drift along sentences
with quick flashes of fins,
questions that shed an impulse
to gather and go somewhere,
diverted by her reedy repetitions to him
of my words, or his to me,
so she becomes the glass we speak through.
A puffer fish when he repeats again
that she's running up my long distance bill,
the elbows of her words grow sharper.
Her goodbye, *in dikke tút*, a big kiss.
He takes the phone again.
Asks, are you still there?
I am.
We begin again the usual water skimming,
everyday vignettes. Mine sing with a riff of sadness
that he interrupts with *fanke, fanke*, girl, girl —
two words which days later I'm still interpreting:
Play, play a little more.
You are as near to me as that.

Arrival: Schiphol

I cross the distance once again —
late night Halifax, dawn over the Atlantic,
blinking at Heathrow's numbered gates,
a fugitive on the run inside my mother's
month-long escapes from her children,
a life she could not leave. She fled

chaos for thirty days at a time:
the pier of Scheveningen ticks
its pendulum into the North Sea
and then cinescape flatness
scored with greenhouse graphs,
straying rivers, and boxy canals.

On the ground, I step into the waiting
mouths of ancestors, their armchairs
and their canonical hours: tea trays
and coffee cups inherited from ravages
and spasmodic joys. Their furniture set
squarely in the eyes of the living.

Meeting My Mother in Rotterdam

Ossip Zadkine, *Verwoeste stad* (1951)

How the war lived on in my mother
I hardly knew — but this statue on the edge
of Rotterdam's water city, found in the drizzle

on a walking tour,
holds my mother's bronze keening. Undefended heart:
an empty hole

where sky gapes, mouth and arms howl.
Five years of occupation after the Germans destroyed
Rotterdam's medieval centre and my mother wore this

like rain the rest of her life.
She was fourteen when the war began
and nineteen when it ended. The war fills

her workbook. Under large numbers 1943
she asks: *Will it bring, like the days of Exodus,*
more sorrow or the end of the plagues?

Near the statue, the new city
a cubist dog, body of blocks, tubes, triangles,
bright colours and dun. My mother crosses

the wide empty space that she traverses sometimes
as the dead will do with the living under changing skies
without regard for which city or country.

Hawthorn

Claws unsheathed, I'm on guard,
mother, for anyone who mishandles
your dismal form.

Nurses empty catheter bags,
roll over your attenuated
limbs. Fingernails gouge my palms

when father sits keening
your name. Quiet-voiced
church women step into this scene

with assurances of a better place,
a freckled aunt in a black
tank top strokes your face, sings

lullabies to light the uncertain way.
Offstage, an orderly asks
Harry for a second time

if he can find his room.
I escape your shallow breathing,
walk away through the back-

drop, clatter down the stairs, surprise
the uncle who just left, standing
by the fire escape, smoking,

his eyes red. Pass a yellow
brick factory, marshy
ditch of jewelweed, hawthorn

trilling with chickadee
song, past a pool with a lone
swimmer, each fingernail

a different opalescence,
and not far from the Driver's Ed
Centre, mishmash of fur-flesh

on the pavement, reeking ugly.
Bedside again, an almost deserted
stage. I avoid father's mute eyes,

stare at his scalp, mottled
under his thin hair, his clavicles
ridge poles inside a shirt tent.

Housekeeping: Portrait of My Father at Eighty-Two

Seated on his cracked vinyl chair, he pours diesel fuel from a plastic bottle onto the wood and lowers the stove covers. The kitchen countertop and electric stove covered with layers of greased dirt, a Vise-Grip, wrench and flathead screwdriver, stacked yogurt containers, crumpled paper towels and newspaper, a microwave unused since the day it was brought in by his brother-in-law. A drain tray has some fairly clean utensils on it and a green glass bowl lying in a brown skim. He shows me the small bag of no-name cat food (only three dollars) that he mixes with other cat food (sold in large bags at the feed mill) for his border collie. Leaning against the wainscotting behind the stove are two feed bags of tin cans, and stacked boxes of wood slats and newspaper. And a pail full of clumps of dog fur. On the table, two blackened newspapers serve as his placemat, next to a jar of peanut butter, a tin of white sandwich cookies, a beer glass half-filled with shadowed sugar. Underneath are stacked crates of condensed milk and more boxes of wood. Moved to where the sideboard used to be, his bed has grey flannel sheets — a gift from a woman at the church. She took the other set away with her to wash. He shows me a statement for $215,000 in GICs at the end of their term — that's one bank. Darkened spiderwebs fringe the cheeseboard hanging on the wall. Cleaning while I cook spaghetti, surfaces reappear. My brother starts the tractor and car and truck to diagnose problems. When my father reaches the end of his questions, he sits eyes closed, legs (sore) stretched out. When we stand up to leave, he says (head down), *I'm glad you came.*

Obdurate, Infirm

This is not a metaphor,
wiry or sharp,
but how he now lives

coffined in one room.
On the floor, acrid
slime and curdled lumps

spill from the wretched
dog's mouth.
The old man's feet are swollen,

red boots, ankle high.
Age backs up his throat,
lungs rasp complaints.

Uncased remains
of a rotary phone:
smashed off the wall

because it rang.
And the few
visitors told

to stop advising
doctor or pills.
They look away

from the body's sloping flesh,
eyes that eat loneliness.

Resurrected Body

You don't get a second chance
with your mother.

But your father's body
returns from the grave of your eyes.

For years, feet only: cowled
socks fallen down over ankle knobs,
red-toed rubber boots manure-
flecked, heavy-soled Sunday shoes,
then corduroy slippers worn
everywhere on pain-rife feet.

Your eyes beggared for years.

His body begins to green
in the mauvest crevices,
a porous sponge-light settled
in his shoulder ridges, hammock
lines of the lower back. You address
his eyes now — no longer seek
some stray limb on the edge
of the field. His psychic tent
no longer has you zippered inside.

There he is, coming into view,
inscrutable, in all his fractured
grandeur.

Stockbridge Cemetery

How these two gravestones bicker
as heat spackles the crevices in the day

and grackles catapult between
the hemlocks. They quarrel

while surrounding granite shines the hours.
Both felt the cutter on the sod, ground

sliced and squared, both heard parents
walk away from their boys sealed in

earth's humusy ears. One stone a knell:
Thy will be done. Hollow pockets

in the air after reverberations end
around his spindle arms and legs.

His little furniture has its place,
toy farm a sprawl of pens —

sheep, goats, and cows. The giraffe,
lion, and hyena stored in his jungle box.

But the other laments *What hopes lie
buried here!* His hair unusually long

because scissors sounded like bleeding to him,
the walls of his room painted black

to let the nightjars in all day.
Angling across the floor a creek,

moss-cushioned rocks.
A corner with quick sand

kept free of chairs, and he always careful
never to step there.

Visitation for an Aunt in Holland

All the time in the world,
she said.
Enough with hurrying out the door
for doctor's appointments, parties, trains.
No more departures.
But you, the internal fire drill
says *find the exits.*
She would give you some of her silence
if you could carry it.

Washed and dressed by her husband
and sons, lipstick lightly applied.
For now, she's chilled
and taken out for family viewing.
Simple fabric trimmed with cord
lines the box where she lies.

One eyelid peeks an eye,
teeth, piano keys at rest.
Your clamouring ebbs in her presence.

You know you belong to sound
above the silence buried here
between hedgerows bordering neighbourly graves.
A few bees still visit sagging floral
arrangements. The horizon rips
as a stealth fighter takes off on a training run
and north of the cemetery
kennelled dogs bark in a hollow room.

And you give yourself up to departure again.
One moment the train waits in the station,

then its ticking wheels pass
graffiti-covered walls, communal garden plots;
you want to watch the city shrink to car size, a cat, a coin,
but the train cuts off the view.

The last word that can never be spoken

He hated his military service, calling it slavery,
yet in his children my father formed
a rigid regiment trained in protocol
for greeting his royal presence:
keep a proper distance, follow orders,
smell them in rising shoulders and snagged gaze;
trained to live like animals in the hollow
between exterior and interior house walls,
stealing warmth and shelter, rarely creeping
into rooms for fear of extinction.
He killed the very idea of goodbye.
Each farewell rattled like an overturned
bin of children's blocks. People approached
his deathbed as if requesting information
from a store clerk. An aunt touched his shoulder
as if testing the ripeness of an avocado.
I tried this too and the avocado
asked, *Are you happy to be my daughter?*
A hesitation, a decision. *Yes.*
While he lay still as death,
mouth sometimes answering, I planned
my goodbye with a random feature:
I would leave when I finished Rilke's *Book of Hours*
(it was my last visit). I would take his hand.
I would say *I love you.* Years of rehearsals
of this moment with a psychiatrist.
Eye to eye with my father's eternal departure,
his body torn to strings, masticated
into pulp by long impacted rage
I ventured out into the middle of the room
with no assurance that I would not kill or be killed.
I closed the book. *I have to go.*

Took his hand, and said what I had to say.
His eyes closed, maybe he smelled tears;
mouth replied, *I'll see you again.*
When I saw him again, his hands were undertaker-folded
on his abdomen, fingers straight except one,
a grasshopper leg about to spring.

Cronus

Not overthrown by his children,
this mortal father
came to his end as many do.
Through hunger's ugly fast,
mouth keeps on eating.
Late learned, not a virtuoso in his yodels
of pain. Uprooted bulbs on dry stalks,
hands shadowbox the wall.
He no longer has eternity in his shoes.
That came and went weeks ago when he wanted
to die but could not, grinding
between reverse and acceleration.
Chug of the portable oxygen machine
takes him down long sleep corridors
on the blanket edge of death.
Sleep cut with riffs of talk.
My hair looks like a stekelbarg—
literally "pinpig," a hedgehog.
Months of toddler incontinence,
mess after mess: he likes the catheter now.
I can just let it all go.
Drug-induced animals occupy the corners,
no threats, just a furry silent fellowship
that might entice him to vacate his room.
Not overthrown in the end, just outlived:
his obituary, his casket, his checkered slippers.

Portrait of My Father after Death

A sign on the edge of a field warns
no crossing without proper documentation
where two countries lie side by side

along a narrow asphalt road
near sleepy villages and vineyards.
Just outside a garden gate

a stray plum tree
split down a crook
into two personas —

one flag-waving-tall,
the other, an unstrung bow.
In the hunched half,

canker and crimes
collar the branches,
long dried into grey-brown ruffs.

Waiting in the shiny leaves
of the laden tree, more fruit
than I could eat

in a casual theft of plums
clouded with surface fog,
fired shades of violet

run up and down
the scales, stopping at a low note
that unhinges the listening throat.

Speed Dating

What would you ask God?
      What kind of question is that?
Do you mean — is it a pick up line?
      Well if it is, could you begin with something less intense?
Could we talk about God's eyebrows?
      We could.
Colour?
      Grey and black with purple streaks.
Shape?
      Of perplexity. Haphazardly bushy. Jolt-like.
Other body parts?
      Toenail.
Which toe?
      The little one on the left foot.
Features?
      Jagged cuticle, nail badly cut, reddish toe.
Other body parts?
      Do you need more?
Not really. Do you have questions?
      Why do your eyebrows twitch when you look to the left?
When I look left, I'm looking at you. . . is that enough?
      Sort of. Do you like ellipses?
Where?
      In punctuation.
I like marks of silence in speech, and places where absence marks
silence.
      Do you prefer the dash?
I like the dashes, square brackets, space between lines, gaps within
lines, page breaks.
      A blank page?
No, the in-between is missing then.

Awry

Flattened your words against your speaking mouth.

— Edna St. Vincent Millay

i.

He showed me Betelgeuse in Orion
from the trampled path that cut
Johnston's Field into snow-crested
triangles; other students passed,
eyes on the icy ground. His look was
everything I wanted. Across the quad,
I watched an emergency crew respond to a false alarm,
quietly packing up the unused equipment.

ii.

In my dormer room, the familiar keeled
clock tower rises beyond row houses.
No visit long enough for my uncle and aunt.
He promised to look me up
on his own travels in Europe. Such long Dutch words —
Ruimtebewapeningswedloop: arms race in space.
I filled a postcard.
Only my name, no address.

iii.

Vinyl-cushioned benches
ring the walls, a smoky den of tippy tables
for chance meetings between classes. On a watercolour day
I brought tête-à-tête daffodils,
placed them beside his coffee cup.
Drenched in my word-storm,
he asks, *what should we do with these?*
I cannot give the gift again, cannot answer, *for you.*

iv.

Interior a stage I managed,
though a stranger kept scraping chairs,
cutting streaks in varnished hardwood.
Secreting myself into the library commons,
waiting to see him,
only once setting on fire
an unknown man's hair —
my incendiary look.

v.

I don't know much about faith, he said.
Sometimes my grandfather took us to church,
almost hitting mailboxes on the way.
My piety only the first domino
in a row of obstacles
I kept setting up and pushing down.
What were the odds that he could tease
threads out of rules I wore vest-tight?

vi.

A summer convocation; on the program, his name
with a middle name I hadn't known. He crossed the rectangular
stage on Johnston's Field. In the press of people after,
our spare words.
I cannot say, *I came for you.*
I fled the roped enclosure to Our Lady on the hill,
leaned on a lacquered wooden back.

Leeuwarden Train Station

A couple meets for the first time
after months of letters.
She, known in her family for her reserve,
hugs him, says he can't meet
her parents now — and light spits
herring scales from a gutter's knife
through iron girders, the sun a fathomless
burn in a muted December sky,
its white light throwing objects
and people into helpless solidity.
Her younger sister died last week.
She will follow him to Canada
and spend most of her years
denying the peculiar cut of his coat,
his character.

Notes

"Unsaying" is borrowed from Michael Sells's book, *Mystical Languages of Unsaying*. Sells translates the Greek term *apophasis* (often used to describe mystical writing reaching toward an elusive God) as "un-saying or speaking-away." Unsaying continually and precariously recreates itself in a vibrant tension with "saying, speaking with" (*kataphasis*).

In the past thirty years efforts have been made to preserve the minority language of Frisian, spoken in Friesland, including the founding of the Fryske Akademy (Frisian Academy) with its dictionary (Dutch-Frisian and Frisian only) and other projects. The Frisian sayings in "Unsaying Poems" are taken from a seventeenth-century collection translated from Middle into Modern Frisian by Frederik Johan van der Kuip in *De Burmania Sprekwurden*. I use van der Kuip's modern Frisian translations; the English translations are my own.

"Jealousy": I owe some of the images to Wim Faber.

"Topsy-Turvy": Jan Steen (1626-1679), Dutch painter and tavern owner.

"Paperpants": I owe the reference to Shonagon to Kaja Silverman in *The Threshold of the Visible World*.

"Three Old Frisian Sisters": The Dutch sometimes refer to ladybugs as *koffee molentjes* (coffee grinders). The poem is a variation on the ghazal form, and in memory of Siem Rutgers-Houtsma.

"The Visit": *Bestemming* is Dutch for destination.

"Looks": Rembrandt's 1658 self-portrait.

"On Not Dying": In memory of Leni Simona Groeneveld.

"Leeuwarden Train Station": Leeuwarden is the capital city of the province of Friesland in the northwest Netherlands.

"Accept Loss": I owe the title and content of the poem to a reflection on the Greg Staats triptych that was exhibited as part of the show "Steeling the Gaze: Portraits by Aboriginal Artists," at the Dalhousie Art Gallery in 2011. The poem is a variation on the nonce form.

"Trespassing" is for I.F.

"Suture": Definitions are taken from the *Canadian Oxford Dictionary*, second edition.

"Meeting my Mother in Rotterdam": The bronze statue *Verwoeste stad* ("Devastated City") was donated by the artist to Rotterdam in the 1950s and remains the city's main war memorial.

"Visitation for an Aunt in Holland": In memory of Tjitske Pander-Houtsma.

"The last word that can never be spoken": The title is taken from a line in the poem "Du bist die Zukunft, grosses Morgenrot" in Rilke's *Book of Hours*.

Acknowledgements

Thank you to the editors of journals in which some of these poems first appeared: the *Antigonish Review*, *Bitterzoet*, *Contemporary Verse 2*, *Ensafh*, the *Fiddlehead*, the *Malahat Review*, and the *Nashwaak Review*.

An earlier version of "Leeuwarden Train Station" (the one-stanza poem) was a finalist in the *Malahat Review* Far Horizons Poetry Prize (2012).

My grateful acknowledgement to the people who, at various stages of my work on this book, were important mentors: Brian Bartlett, John Barton, Anne Carson, Anne Compton, Sue Goyette, Carole Langille, Kathleen Skerrett, and, at our regular monthly meetings, the Dublin Street poets (Rose Adams, Brian Braganza, John McLeod, and Marilynn Rudi). My sincere thanks to Ross Leckie, my editor, for his many styles of keen editorial engagement with my poems, and to the board and editors at Goose Lane for believing in this project and making it a better book. And to David Heckerl for unending sustenance.

photo: Massimo Pedrazzini

Dust or Fire is Alyda Faber's first book of poetry. Her poems have appeared in Canadian literary magazines and online journals, as well as in a chapbook, *Berlinale Erotik: Berlin Film Festival*. She teaches Systematic Theology and Ethics at the Atlantic School of Theology in Halifax.